VOLUNTEERING:

SKILLS THAT LAST YOU A LIFETIME

BECOME THE ENTREPRENEUR THAT
CHANGES LIVES

By: Jay Williamson

Table of Contents

Acknowledgements

It is truly wonderful, the amazing people that I have in my life, that know me for me, and still provides me the kind of love, friendship and support that is hard to find. Who would have thought that just a year ago, it never crossed my mind to be an author, but with the individuals that I have around me, I can do nothing but grow and go higher. I would like to give a special thanks to my wife Ilana for her constant patience, love, and support! My love, you always give me a warm smile; you always encourage me; you always lift me up and tell me that I can do anything and words will never be able to express my gratitude for you making such a positive difference in my life. Thank you to my Parents who raised me to have a heart to give and hands to help. Thank you to the C.R.E.A.T.E. Your Book Now Blueprint creator and the C.R.E.A.T.E. leadership… to you Subira Folami for your leadership, guidance and patience; to you Sensei David Sztajer for your great ideas and checking up on us in your group. To my book buddies, Ursula Young, and Nancy Evans , who although you were far ahead of me in the process, you kept reaching back and pulling me forward. To J. L. Bumbrey, who , although I tell him all the time, still doesn't realize how much of an influence he has been in my life. And last but not least… to my Grandmother Mary Coleman, you always had a heart to help people. It is your heart that lives on in me.

A Special Note About How This Book Was Intentionally Created:

Dear Family of Volunteers, this book was initially created from a live interview. That's why it reads like a conversation rather than the traditional "book" that talks "at" you.

I wanted you to feel as though I'm talking "with" you much like a close friend or relative.

I felt that creating the book this way would make it easier for you to grasp the topics and put them to use quickly rather than waiting through hundreds of pages.

So relax.

Grab a pen or pencil and some paper. Take notes and get ready to learn how to become the entrepreneur that changes lives.

Sincerely,
Jay Williamson

CHAPTER 1:

Jay Williamson, Life-long Volunteer Expert and Entrepreneur That's Changing Lives

Good evening and welcome everyone to the informational guide that takes you through the step-by-step ways of becoming an entrepreneur by using skills already possessed by those who are volunteers.

Jay Williamson is somewhat of a professional volunteer and he is an expert on the subject of volunteering and has recently written a book called Volunteering: Skills That Last You a Lifetime, and I think this is really intriguing.

INTERVIEWER: So Jay is a well-known expert and he's been volunteering for years, which you will hear about later as the interview progresses, and he's going to be sharing with us the state of the union, what exactly is happening on the landscape of volunteerism and how he has been able to translate these skill sets into business. And also, the advantages that volunteers have by doing that. He's going to be talking to us about the leverage that volunteering has on business and how volunteers have more skills than they realize to become entrepreneurs. Now tell us a little bit about that, what were some of your earliest memories of volunteering?

JAY WILLIAMSON: Well, my earliest memory of when I got into the field volunteering was really with just the things that I was doing on my own as a young child. First of all, I developed a heart to volunteer when I was 8 years old. I went on a school field trip to a nursing facility, of which my mom was a chaperone. I remember as a little boy we were taking and passing out balloons and visiting the elderly people.It's still so fresh that I can recall it like yesterday, the feeling of just seeing the smiles on their faces. This really affected what I really wanted to do with my life. So it was from there that I started. My dad was a department store manager for K-mart, and we moved every year and a half to two years from the time that I was born. So from that time at that nursing home, every time we would pick up and move to another city, I would always find some elderly person in our neighborhood and I would go and sit with them, talk to them and listen to their stories. From there something was planted inside of me and it developed into me doing some heavy lifting around their houses, or maybe even mowing their lawns. When I was old enough to drive, I would run errands for them and even take them to the grocery stores. So that was what I was doing on my own until I started volunteering for organizations.

INTERVIEWER: Wow, okay, that's a long time of volunteering. Now did you have, within those organizations, formal training in volunteering or has it all been kind of on the job training?

JAY WILLIAMSON: Once I joined an organization, I always received formal training by going through orientation and getting specified training depending on what I was doing. Then after my orientation, I would get training out in the field.

INTERVIEWER: Okay, so over the course of time, tell me a little bit more about some of the skill sets that you have acquired as volunteer that translate over to business.

JAY WILLIAMSON: Well, there's so much that I formally learned and was formally trained in when I started joining non-profit organizations. I have learned communication skills. I've learned customer service skills.

I've learned listening skills. I've been a part of organizations where I've had to learn how to negotiate.

INTERVIEWER: Tell me about that, why would a volunteer need to learn to negotiate?

JAY WILLIAMSON: I was a part of an organization called CASA, which stood for Court Appointed Special Advocate for abused and neglected children. My duty was to visit the children that I was assigned to, who were taken out of their homes because of neglect or abuse. What I had to do was to report back to the court and the judge exactly what the wishes of each child was. I did not only deal with the children, but I dealt with their parents too, I had to deal with lawyers as well as with social workers and sometimes nurses and doctors. So inside and outside the courtroom, I had to try to negotiate to either get that child back into his or her home with their parents or to find them a safe environment as fast as possible.

INTERVIEWER: Okay, okay, so negotiation is definitely a skill set that we need as an entrepreneur. And so how has that helped you in your business?

JAY WILLIAMSON: You know, working in business, you're negotiating all the time, there are times when things seem to be going back and forth and there's a give and take that you're always doing in business especially when you're dealing with people one on one. So I have used that skill to help me as an entrepreneur.

INTERVIEWER: Okay, cool, have you ever had a situation where your business negotiation was as sensitive as any of your cases. I would probably assume some of these case negotiations had to be sensitive, since if I would imagine that negotiating for a child to get the best that they need in an environment that had previously and might still be detrimental to them to negotiate on their behalf to be their voice. I'm just trying to find the cross over. If you can think of any situations in business, where you've had sensitive negotiations.

JAY WILLIAMSON: Well, I can't say that I've had a sensitive negotiation such as trying to get a child back into the home with their parents, but when you're dealing with people and you're trying to get them to buy a service or product, It's sensitive in that fashion. If you think about it, all negotiating is sensitive to whoever the customer is, with whatever their needs are and with whatever they're looking to buy. I have to be able to delicately bring that person into the sales environment to see that what they're looking for, is what I have.

INTERVIEWER: So, what I'm hearing you say is that you've been in a situation when you're negotiating, whether it's for a child or for an older person, that you get to be that person's voice and you make sure that both parties get what they need, but your primary objective was to make sure that your client got what they needed.

JAY WILLIAMSON: That is correct.

CHAPTER 2:

You Have The Right Skills: Looking To The Internet To Get Started

INTERVIEWER: So tell me what are some gradual changes, you've seen over time, that will help volunteers that are looking for a way to be free to follow their passions? What are some things that you've noticed?

JAY WILLIAMSON: Well, one of the things that I have noticed that has changed over time, and which I believe will help volunteers to begin the process of becoming free to pursue their passions by becoming entrepreneurs is with the advent of the internet.

INTERVIEWER: Please, say more about that, what do you mean?

JAY WILLIAMSON: What I'm saying is the old way of trying to become an entrepreneur was almost exclusive to those who had good contacts and a lot of startup capital to invest in opening a business. With the internet, now you can run a business virtually, and in a lot of cases, right from the palm of your hand using your cell phone. Also, there's no need for high overhead. Getting started online with a business can be affordable, and is rather simple, but some expenses are necessary. For example, if you have a good idea for a product or service, you would like to get into the marketplace, you can start with a business website, for as low as $2.75 per month, which to me is absolutely incredible considering that business startup costs can run pretty high - a study from the Kauffman Foundations shows the average cost to be at least $30,000, and costs tend to increase each year. Furthermore, you'll need to pay for custom web design, which could cost you a few hundred dollars if you want to hire a professional to do this work for you. That's only if you have a specific brand and your following branding standards. However, if you hire a professional, he/she will use your brand colors and fonts to design your menus, homepage and the other content on your site. But all this is not necessary at the beginning when you're first starting up. If you don't adhere to certain brand standards, you can potentially find a free website theme online to add to your site.

INTERVIEWER: And so with that, how does that translate into marketing?

JAY WILLIAMSON: With the onset of everything going online, volunteers desiring to become entrepreneurs can use a process that is more modernized to market. The old way of marketing to someone, which again cost a lot of money, was by putting a bunch of flyers on bulletin boards, and maybe the occasional radio interview, that was just a plea on how to get someone to buy, and that is outdated and fast becoming a thing of the past. Now what has developed is the highlight on social media marketing. For example, say a volunteer that wants to be a freelance data entry worker. There is this volunteer engagement website called VolunteerMatch which is the largest volunteer website of its kind. LinkedIn has a volunteer marketplace that can opt into this website. One fascinating thing about LinkedIn being able to integrate into VolunteerMatch is that if a person pins any of their skills into the VolunteerMatch opportunity, that skill or skills will be cross-posted on LinkedIn's volunteer marketplace. The benefit is that that simply gives entrepreneurs a wider exposure as far as who they can match themselves, their product, or their services up to as far as the marketplace.

INTERVIEWER: Okay, so what you're saying is that if I'm on LinkedIn, and VolunteerMatch integrates with LinkedIn, then I can list my skill sets or what I have to offer, and this website VolunteerMatch matches my skills or whatever services I have to offer with all those who are looking for similar services? Then it lets me know, or lets the marketplace know, or how does that work?

JAY WILLIAMSON: Yes, It works both ways. VolunteerMatch being integrated with LinkedIn, lets the marketplace see what you have to offer and they also will let the freelance volunteer know.

INTERVIEWER: Awesome, okay. And now does it do this for people who are looking for volunteers with certain skill sets? Do I have to say in my bio that I'm a freelancer looking to offer certain services, or my LinkedIn bio doesn't mention my skill sets? Would I still be somehow matched up with marketplace opportunities, or do I have to actually put what opportunities I'm available for?

JAY WILLIAMSON: Yes, you definitely want to put in your bio as many skill sets as possible to increase your chances of being selected for your freelance work. You also want to put what freelance jobs you are willing to do.

INTERVIEWER: Oh okay, so I have a profile on VolunteerMatch and I also have my profile on LinkedIn?

JAY WILLIAMSON: Yes, and when my skill sets match what someone is looking for, I'll be notified, or I can look for certain freelance jobs that match my skill sets and offer my services in a bid if the opportunity needs to be bid for. So that eliminates my need to go out and actually solicit places to freelance because this website integration does it for me.

CHAPTER 3:

The State Of Volunteers Becoming Entrepreneurs

INTERVIEWER: So tell me how would you characterize the state of volunteers becoming entrepreneurs today?

JAY WILLIAMSON: When it comes to volunteers who have a desire to become entrepreneurs, in most cases there are similar aspects of life that are holding them back. You see, 2 problems have existed for some time that many people are convinced that it is not suitable to commit to the process of becoming an entrepreneur. First, the lack of time is a dominant influence that prevents a lot from taking action as a volunteer. And the second reason is having to take care of young children or family. With both of these reasons, most people are waiting for things to calm down in their lives, which in most cases it never does. It's because of these situations, in which many find challenging to overcome, that being able to start your business online and becoming an entrepreneur is easier than it ever has been.

INTERVIEWER: Why would you say that it's easier now to become an entrepreneur than before?

JAY WILLIAMSON: Well, as I've stated before, the startup cost to become an entrepreneur can be ridiculously low. But there are many more benefits and advantages that a volunteer has that makes it uncomplicated for volunteers to get started sooner than later.

INTERVIEWER: And so explain to me or give me some insight as to what is the advantage for me if I'm a volunteer and I want to get started, but feel like I lack the knowledge or skills of an entrepreneur.

JAY WILLIAMSON: There are so many more benefits to volunteering than what most people are thinking about. What is most people's perception of volunteering? Most people think that volunteering is just a chance to help your local community or lend a hand in some way. There's much more to being a volunteer than just thinking about others or trying to be selfless. Volunteering often helps the volunteer in more ways than the people or projects that they support.

INTERVIEWER: Please could you elaborate more on.

JAY WILLIAMSON: Okay… Want a better understanding of what your own abilities are? A great way to get that understanding is through volunteering. A fantastic way to understand how to accomplish something new is by getting involved. Whether you're helping to plan a huge event or making flyers for a small gathering, every task great or small can be beneficial to you in this way. I read that The United Nations has a volunteering organization that they call the UN volunteers, and this is what they say, "volunteering is the perfect vehicle to discover something you are really good at and develop a new skill."

INTERVIEWER: Have you discovered some of your abilities by being a volunteer?

JAY WILLIAMSON: Absolutely!

INTERVIEWER: Please share some of what you learned.

JAY WILLIAMSON: Yes. I learned many things when I was volunteering with the organization CASA. I keep going back to CASA because that was the very first non-profit organization that I joined. I actually had to go through orientation, and I had to be trained to do what I was going to be doing. I learned so many valuable skills with CASA. For these particular volunteering assignments, I had to have negotiating skills, I had to have communication and listening skills.Also, I was on the board of CASA and through joining the board, I really learned organizational skills. This involved learning about how an organization's finances worked. So with this I learned about fundraising, and how to incorporate that into trying to get more sponsors and resources.You see, I learned big skills like how to plan and budget and how to supervise and manage. Also, I was able to enhance the skills I already had by spending more time actively using them.

INTERVIEWER: So what you are saying is that there were skills that you already had that you were able to add to and increase, just by continuing your volunteer experience? I would like to hear more about that.

JAY WILLIAMSON: I have a great example from my experience learning to be a negotiator. I first learned basic skills as a negotiator when I was with the non-profit organization that I keep mentioning, which is C.A.S.A.

INTERVIEWER: And C.A.S.A. stands for what again?

JAY WILLIAMSON: I was a Court Appointed Special Advocate for abused and neglected children. I had to be trained on how to interact with the children's parents, who obviously wanted their children back home. I had to negotiate with social workers, lawyers, and sometimes doctors, not to mention the children who I represented in court. I became a very good representative for the children I was speaking for. Out of the 8 cases that I had, I was able to get 7 of the children back home with their parents. Well, this training came in handy when I became a UAW Union Representative. My skills as a negotiator were greatly enhanced after I became a union rep. This was way more than trying to help children, I was either fighting to save someone's job or trying to get their job back. Out of the 9 cases that I was over, I was successfully able to save 8 jobs. This was also due to some part of the training that I had obtained from C.A.S.A.

INTERVIEWER: This is really good information. Is there any other advantages to being a volunteer that would help your audience to begin the process of becoming an entrepreneur?

JAY WILLIAMSON: Yes actually… Just 2 more things that I would like to mention. One thing is that if you want a great way to network, volunteering is a great opportunity to meet new people. Many volunteers are former big business people or big players in the business world. Volunteering is just their way of giving back. I've met former doctors, nurses, and lawyers that are now volunteers in my organization. But with volunteering, I believe the diversity of people you can meet through volunteering has a different face than anywhere else.

INTERVIEWER: How do you mean?

JAY WILLIAMSON: This is what I am trying to say. Volunteering is a way to greatly broaden your horizons because many diverse people volunteer throughout every community, so having the opportunity to meet and speak with them can give you new information and ways of looking at the world with an educational difference. Also, If you want a great sense of fulfillment... give back in the form of volunteering. You can improve your own self-esteem and confidence through your skills and help improve your community. You can do this by accomplishing something you never thought you could. In a nutshell, volunteering is more than just a way to boost your experience for an application. The things you can learn and give back will last you a long time and will act as a foundation to build upon for the rest of your life.

INTERVIEWER: Ok, I see that being a part of a volunteer organization is the perfect vehicle to acquire a lot of skills necessary for any business. You are really good at explaining this topic... And also to develop new skills, and I would probably say just leadership in general. Would you agree there?

JAY WILLIAMSON: Absolutely!

CHAPTER 4:

Overcoming The Challenges Of Becoming An Entrepreneur

INTERVIEWER: Ok, so what are the biggest challenges right now that, volunteers who want to become entrepreneurs but feel they lack the skills, are going to face right now?

JAY WILLIAMSON: Almost all challenges tend to fall into the same two areas regardless of the geographical location, or the types of communities or initiatives anyone serves: money and time. When it comes to money, the challenge is not only how to find the funds to start up your business, but it's also how to keep yourself in business for the long-term. Although most online businesses require little capital to get started, there is the monthly cost of running your business. Things like marketing platforms, auto-responders, mentorship or coaching are necessary, if you will be successful over time. Some things like marketing, training, and some coaching you can find online for free. But you eventually have to pay if you want to take your business to the next level.

INTERVIEWER: Okay, that makes sense, what about the time aspect?

JAY WILLIAMSON: As crucial as time management is, you can find yourself in a difficult position if you are just starting a business. What makes it even more difficult is if you have a daily routine and you are used to running your own schedule. Now to me, the biggest challenge of all, which is a major one across the nation, is the time management balance issue. It's challenging having the time to be able to balance home life, being a volunteer and committing to starting up as an entrepreneur. Over time, like any accomplished entrepreneur realizes, it can become very difficult to maintain a work-life-business balance, not to mention your volunteering a few hours a week. After a while, you can become so overwhelmed that you neglect the responsibilities you have for other areas of your life. Then you become manic about work and business-related tasks, working from sun up to sun down just to get things crossed off your list. Then what's neglected next is good eating habits, proper sleep, and family life.

INTERVIEWER: Wow! That sounds really serious! Do you even have a solution to these challenges?

JAY WILLIAMSON: Actually, as serious as these challenges sound, I do have a workable solution.

INTERVIEWER: Please do share.

JAY WILLIAMSON: Basically, I've already explained about the money situation. You can start offline as a network marketer and easily take your business online. You can go online and do affiliate marketing or e-commerce. You can do freelance work by providing data entry, content writing, or administrative work. If you like graphic design, you can do that as well. You can even open an online store using eBay, Amazon, or Shopify. The list of ways to start is endless, and it doesn't take tens or hundreds of thousands of dollars to get started. Now when starting with any of these businesses, you can practically do all you need for free if you want to take the time to do so to save a little money. Eventually, you will need to pay a little money to automate your growing customer list like an autoresponder. YouTube is like the new university. You can find free training on anything you want that pertains to your particular business, to help you with the learning curve.

INTERVIEWER: I see what you're saying about money, but if a person is busy and don't have a lot of time just because of the basic areas of life, how will someone deal with that aspect?

JAY WILLIAMSON: I definitely agree with you, but if people want to one day fully give themselves to what their passion is and they are serious about getting started on that path, dealing with the time aspect is very doable. I'm not only speaking about what I've seen others do, but I'm speaking from my own experience. I'm not only an entrepreneur, but I work full time, I take care of my family, and I volunteer on average from 1 to 5 hours a week, visiting and sitting with hospice patients. At a time when I had up to 8 patients at once, I have seen tremendous results in my business. At that same time I was pulling in more leads per day that I had ever done in business before. So I know this works. How do I have a great time management balance? Well, this what a mentor of mine calls, the 'Nooks and Crannies' of your day. Once I saw and understood this concept, and applied it, my time to do everything I needed to do opened right up. It was amazing! And it works! This is all I did: I took those little moments of the day that most people use doing anything else, and I made them times of production. When I took a 10-15 break, I would create a post. On my 30 minute lunch, I would engage with my target audience. If I had to go to the restroom, if I got stopped by a train, even if my son and I were out having fun, I would find those small increments of time to do a little business. All this was during the same time I was visiting 8 patients, working a full-time job, taking care of my family, and the leads were pouring in and my customer list was growing every day.

INTERVIEWER: Ok, it really sounds like you have the experience to back up what you are talking about. So how much time would most non-profit organizations like from people when they volunteer in your estimate?

JAY WILLIAMSON: It will depend on what type of volunteering you are involved with. I'm sure it varies from organization to organization. I'm volunteering with an organization right now called JourneyCare. Like I said, I was up to at least eight patients a week that I was a Care Companion for. I would see those patients 30 minutes at a time throughout each week. But, you know, I had that many patients, and there was still a whole list of patients that didn't have volunteers most likely because of the time aspect, and most people do not have the time to drive somewhere and volunteer for 30 minutes to an hour, and then drive back. Now, imagine trying to start as an entrepreneur or business owner. This is not for the faint of heart. That's why I'm specifically talking to volunteers who have a heart and passion to volunteer. I'm talking to volunteers that have made it their lives to give to others and are seeking for a way to eventually be able to give more time to what they love to do.

CHAPTER 5:

Using Your Skills To Take Advantage Of The Big Opportunities

INTERVIEWER: Where are the big opportunities in the beginning as an entrepreneur that volunteers might be missing?

JAY WILLIAMSON: A lot of volunteers don't realize the source of ideas that they come into contact with every day as a volunteer that could be a catalyst for starting as an entrepreneur. Say for instance, if you're a medical student and you want to follow your passion in medicine and you get some experience by becoming a volunteer at the hospital, you would be surrounded by a wealth of information and ideas, as well as a network of people in the area you love. You have the opportunity to come up with ideas, products or services that would help you serve others as an entrepreneur. If you're going to school to be a teacher, or some kind of educator you can volunteer at a school. The same, for example, goes for anyone who volunteers in an area that they are passionate about.

INTERVIEWER: So the opportunities are endless. That's awesome! So what you're saying is that anything you are remotely interested in as a volunteer, you can as well come up with an entrepreneurial idea for. So let's say, for instance, you can go down to the pet store, and volunteer as a dog training assistant. You could have the idea to sell something for puppies, as an entrepreneur, or you could develop your own program to teach people how to make their pets behave. Okay, so you're basically saying that as a volunteer, it would be an advantage for me to look for an idea, product or service that would compliment me as an entrepreneur in the field that I'm passionate about?

JAY WILLIAMSON: Yes, that is exactly right.

INTERVIEWER: Okay, so what major events or developments do you see in the immediate future, for volunteers who want to become entrepreneurs but feel they lack the skills?

JAY WILLIAMSON: It's obvious that all new entrepreneurs, when launching their first business are inexperienced. What they need to do rather quickly in the beginning is to draw on someone else's experience. The best way to overcome this inexperience quickly, is by engaging in a mentorship or advisor programs. So the first step in finding a mentor is to recognize the importance of asking for help and being open to external feedback. Mentors are the way to achieve this. Again, the internet just makes finding a mentor so easy. Just a few ways to find a mentor is by going to networking events, entrepreneur 'hot spots', LinkedIn and Twitter, small business development centers (SBDCs), industry centers, indirect competitors, and my favorite, a volunteer organization called SCORE.

INTERVIEWER: Wait a minute, A volunteer organization. I thought you were talking about finding a mentor.

JAY WILLIAMSON: Exactly! That's why I like this way of finding a mentor for volunteers. They are my favorite because its volunteers who are dedicated to helping volunteers and individuals start, run and grow their own businesses. I think that is absolutely incredible! Through SCORE, you can request a free face-to-face meeting with a mentor to discuss your business idea -- and you may be able to form a more lasting partnership. This is what SCORE says about their vision and their mission. "(We) help make dreams come true. Every year, SCORE volunteers help thousands of entrepreneurs start small businesses and achieve new levels of success. Volunteering is a way for you to give back, network with business experts, and share your knowledge." Isn't that great?

INTERVIEWER: Yes, that's always nice to have. See if I'm a volunteer and I have a big heart, I would want to be in a supportive community, in whatever area that I'm interested in. But at the same time, I don't want to be slowed down, because of lack of technology because I got to get back to work or spend time with my family, or just kick my feet up, which can be difficult for us to find time to do so. So it's good to know that technology is making it easier to get the help we need to be successful in becoming an entrepreneur. You mentioned mentorship being necessary for anyone becoming an entrepreneur. Did you have mentors that were a help to you starting a business?

JAY WILLIAMSON: Yes I did. In fact, I have had several mentors and coaches. I have a mentor and a coach right now. I attribute my current success to having these individuals in my life.

INTERVIEWER: So where do you see volunteers who want to become entrepreneurs but feel they lack the skills so will make mistakes?

JAY WILLIAMSON: The biggest mistake that I feel volunteers make in not pursuing becoming entrepreneurs is the very thought that they lack the skills necessary to start a business. As I have demonstrated, volunteers are using the necessary skills every day when they put their volunteer hat on their heads.

INTERVIEWER: Yeah, I can see that. You have explained that very clearly. Is there anything else they are missing?

JAY WILLIAMSON: Yes, another mistake volunteers make is when they think that they have to start a business by themselves. There are more support groups, and more online as well as offline help that a new entrepreneur can get involved in. Even if a new entrepreneur can't necessarily afford to pay for mentorship right away, there are many people willing to give help and advice on blogs, forums, and Facebook groups. The help is always there, you just have to look for it.

INTERVIEWER: Okay, so you have to really want it. This is why you want to become an entrepreneur in an area that is closest to your volunteer experience. So who are the people that are the movers, and the shakers right now in the arena of entrepreneurial start-ups. And what specific areas do you see to be needing a little bit shaking up in the near future or already have an impact?

JAY WILLIAMSON: Well, I don't know of any specific individuals making big moves, but there are companies that have created a huge online presence with their products and services, and they are providing assistance to new entrepreneurs (as well as veterans) to help them get started and to build their businesses. For example, Amazon is definitely a mover and shaker in the online space. Amazon is the most popular online retailer in the United States, beating out eBay, Walmart and Target. Amazon has one of the most powerful (and least well-known) tools for trending market research - and believe it or not, it's called the Amazon Movers and Shakers list. What the Movers and Shakers list does is help entrepreneurs to stay one step ahead of the competition. It does this by taking the knowledge of how to find what products are trending on Amazon, and helps the entrepreneur to translate this knowledge into more sales. This is a huge help to up and coming entrepreneurs to take advantage of. Using the Movers and Shakers list gives entrepreneurs a big head start of the competition.

CHAPTER 6:

The Science Behind Why Volunteers Are Ready To Begin Right Now

INTERVIEWER: Any final thoughts there? Anything else that I haven't asked you about volunteers who want to become entrepreneurs but lack the skills that you think is important to be addressed, before, we close up your book?

JAY WILLIAMSON: Yes, just one aspect that I really would like to mention. It's how being a volunteer affects you from a scientific standpoint and gives the volunteer an advantage that can be easily transferred into being an entrepreneur that people will know, like, and trust. You see, there is a neurotransmitter called dopamine that when it's released in the brain, it improves your overall sense of well-being and increases your capacity to learn, to be creative, and experience increased levels of vibrancy, all inner skills that any good entrepreneur needs in business. You experience the effects of dopamine when you feel happier, then you are more willing to learn, and you also reduce stress more effectively. It has been scientifically proven that helping people makes you feel good. Therefore, volunteering helps you feel good about making a difference in the world, and when volunteers become entrepreneurs, they already have the experience of being happy and upbeat and are a lot more pleasant to deal with and more productive. Just one more thing. When you volunteer, you give yourself opportunities to meet business leaders, politicians and other entrepreneurs who can help you take your small business to the next level. Now, how is this? Because volunteering is all about adopting a "give back" attitude — and you're almost certain to meet someone who can benefit you — or someone who you can benefit. Either way, you've just made a new contact and potential friends! I really hope that it can be seen how being a volunteer already provides a person with the necessary skills to start any venture as an entrepreneur.

INTERVIEWER: Nice, okay cool, well thank you so much for a great interview. You have definitely shined a new light on that relationship between volunteerism and being an entrepreneur, and for those of us like myself, who do have a helpers heart, I hope that it's understood that there are a lot of advantages volunteers have and that they shouldn't hesitate to follow their passions and dreams in life. So thank you very much for bringing a clear understanding to volunteers for that and I appreciate that. I also want to thank all of the readers of this book for taking the time to join in the community that you are creating of volunteers who actually want to incorporate being an entrepreneur into their passion for the pursuit of their dreams. I think that's unique and I think it's needed, especially how he started at the top of this, with his own experience and how he acquired many skills that easily translated into being an entrepreneur, and the lessons he learned along the way. So thanks for bringing all this to light. I think this was a really great conversation and I know that this is going to be an enjoyable book, and I'm excited to see what you do with it beyond even just the book. So thank you so much for taking the time to share this part of your life with us.

JAY WILLIAMSON: You're welcome and thank you.